I0473144

7 Steps To Keep Your Loved One Safe In A Nursing Home

by

Brad Lakin

Brad Lakin

You are not permitted to copy, broadcast, use for commercial purposes, show or play in public, adapt or change in any way the content of these web pages for any other purpose whatsoever without the prior written permission of the author.

This book was written to provide families with valuable information regarding nursing homes. It is not intended to be "Advertising Material," but the information contained herein may be considered advertising material by some.

The author and publisher do not make any representations or warranties regarding the accuracy of the information contained herein and specifically disclaim all warranties, including without limitation warranties of fitness for a particular purpose.

Nothing in this book is intended to be legal advice. The author and his firm do not provide legal advice unless there is a written representation agreement. Please understand that your legal matter, if one exists, is unique, different and like no others. Likewise, each jurisdiction has statutes of limitations that impose time limitations for when legal claims may be brought. If you need legal advice, you should consult with a qualified attorney about your specific situation, and never rely on this book or any other book for that matter.

Brad Lakin

WHY THIS BOOK? ....Page 5

GETTING STARTED ....Page 11

ENSURE GOOD NURSING HOME CARE ....Page 11

STEP 1: BE A ZEALOUS & VIGILANT ADVOCATE
....Page 12

STEP 2: THE PLAN OF CARE – THE RECIPE!
....Page 13

STEP 3: CONTINUE TO MONITOR THE FACILITY
....Page 14

STEP 4: SUPPORT THE STAFF ....Page 15

STEP 5: COMMUNICATE & COMMUNICATE MORE
....Page 16
Improving Communication ....Page 17
When Problems Occur ....Page 17
File a CONFIDENTIAL Complaint if Necessary...Page 18

STEP 6: KEEP TRACK OF INSPECTIONS ....Page 21

STEP 7: THE NEWSPAPER TRAIL ....Page 24

HELPFUL RESOURCES ....Page 25

NURSING HOME CHECKLISTS ....Page 26
Nursing Home Checklist ....Page 26
Nursing Home Review Checklist ....Page 34

KNOW THE RESIDENT'S RIGHTS ....Page 36

NURSING HOME RESIDENT RIGHTS ....Page 36

1

Brad Lakin

GENERAL GOALS OF THE LAW......................Page 38
Quality of Life...Page 38
Provision of Services and Activities ....Page 38
Participation in Home Administration ....Page 38
Access to the Ombudsman Program ....Page 39

SPECIFIC RESIDENT RIGHTS............................Page 40
Rights to Self-Determination ....Page 40
Personal and Privacy Rights ....Page 40
Rights Regarding Abuse and Restraints................Page 41
Rights to Information..Page 42
Right to Visits ....Page 43
Transfer and Discharge Rights..............................Page 43
Protection of Personal Funds ....Page 45
Protection Against Medicaid Discrimination..........Page 46

WHO TO CONTACT RESOURCES.....................Page 47

OMBUDSMEN..Page 48

CITIZEN GROUPS ....Page 66

NURSING HOME ABUSE HOTLINES ....Page 79

About the Author

Brad Lakin, Esq. is a best-selling author who has been inducted into the *National Academy of Best Selling Authors* and a trial lawyer who is often sought out by media to discuss his clients' cases. Brad has appeared on ABC, CBS, NBC, FOX affiliates, and CNN, and has been quoted and highlighted in newspapers throughout the country.

Brad has repeatedly been recognized by his peers as a *Super Lawyer*, a *Rising Star*, one of *America's Premier Experts®* and in 2006 as one of *Forty Lawyers Under Forty to Watch*. He has also been honored as a *Top 100 Trial Lawyer* by *The National Trial Lawyers*, a nationwide organization. These honors stem from his success as a litigator in the courtroom.

In a 2005 product liability trial, Lakin helped his clients win a $43 million victory – the second largest verdict in Illinois and the 30th nationwide. The case was a featured story throughout the country and included an appearance on CNN's Anderson Cooper 360. Brad has tried cases to verdict in Illinois, Oklahoma, Arkansas, West Virginia, Nebraska, Missouri, and Ohio.

During the course of his career, his firms have represented clients in all 50 states.

Brad's passion for nursing home abuse cases stems from a personal tragedy that happened to a member of his family. Brad's goal in his work and for this book is to prevent the same type of tragedy from happening to others. Brad is known nationally for his successful courtroom advocacy in personal injury, mass torts, and a variety of complex litigation matters.

His firm has recovered over $700 million in verdicts, settlements, and benefits for their clients. To learn more about Brad Lakin and his firm, visit www.GreatInjuryLawyers.com or call (800) 550-2106.

WHY THIS BOOK?

Betty [her real name changed for privacy] was recently admitted to a local nursing home. She experienced frequent episodes of elopement from her home. People with dementia often try to leave their secure environment. She started to do things like leave the oven on. To protect Betty, her loving family decided to start looking for a nursing home facility somewhere close for family visits.

They started in the Yellow Pages with nursing homes in the area and went and visited a few. When they arrived on the scheduled day to visit the facility, it "looked good" — the administration staff was friendly and inviting; there were plenty of staff wandering the halls; and beds were available. Everything "looked good," so the family admitted Betty shortly thereafter.

If you didn't read my book, *How to Select a Nursing Home for a Loved One*, this is exactly what you would do. In fact, it's precisely what thousands of loving and caring family members and friends do for their loved ones every year.

On admission day, everything "looked good" to an untrained eye. As days passed, Betty was active in the facility. Of course she was slipping mentally, but she enjoyed visits from family, participated in daily activities like arts and crafts, and was able to walk freely within the facility. Months into her stay at the nursing home, Betty wandered from the facility – just as she had at home. The staff later acknowledged, and her medical records mentioned, that Betty was always saying, "I want to go home."

How In The World Could This Happen?

Betty wandered out the back door where an auditory safety alarm had been removed from the door months prior.

Most nursing homes have a safety alarm system known as Wanderguard®. A safety bracelet is worn by residents who are at risk of leaving the facility and have a history of wandering like Betty's. The door she left through didn't have Wanderguard® for a good reason – because the door allowed her and other residents to exit the building into a SECURE fenced-in courtyard where they could enjoy the outdoors.

Back to the actual door: It had an audible alarm that would signal when a resident left so staff would know when Betty, or someone else was going outside. But, it was removed because it apparently "bothered" some staff members or administrators. Unfortunately for Betty, it was never replaced despite repeated requests to the administration. These requests fell on deaf ears.

...The Courtyard Was Secured By A Fence, Right?

Wrong. The gate had been physically removed from its hinges and was leaning up against the fence. The as-advertised "secure and safe courtyard" turned out to be the final straw. Betty escaped by walking out the back exit. About 75 feet down the sidewalk she fell and struck her head on the cement, where she remained for anywhere from 35 minutes to 2.5 hours. No one truly knew how long she remained on the ground because none of the staff noticed she was gone until she was found lying injured on the pavement.

Betty was rushed to a nearby hospital where an MRI revealed she had suffered a subdural hematoma (bleeding on the brain). For anyone, this is a serious brain injury. For the elderly, it's typically catastrophic. It was for Betty. She never recovered. She lost her independence...her ability to walk. She never walked again.

Brad Lakin

The Phone Call

I was two years out of law school, over 13 years ago, when I first learned about nursing home neglect. It began when Betty's daughter called my office and spoke to one of my staff members. Betty's daughter had been referred to another local lawyer, because at the time, we were not handling nursing home neglect cases. We are big believers in only concentrating in areas where we have significant experience. Although our firm had extensive experience with injury law, we did not handle nursing home neglect cases at the time.

A few days later, upon returning home from work one evening, I received a call from my mother-in-law questioning me about why our office turned down Aunt Betty's case. I had never met Aunt Betty. So, I circled back with my staff and learned the facts. Boy was that call a punch in the gut. I just knew that no one would pour their heart and soul into Aunt Betty's case like I would, no matter how experienced they were.

It was at that moment I committed myself to learning anything and everything to help Aunt Betty. After all, she wanted to go home but the family didn't have money to provide around-the-clock care. So, I called the local lawyer who'd taken her case and explained the situation. He graciously understood and we took over.

"If I Only Knew"

Roughly a year later we were preparing for trial. After hours upon hours of preparation and depositions, I sat down with Betty's daughter to explain what we had uncovered ... essentially the facts I mentioned above and more. Her response, "If I only knew!" meant, "If I only knew about the nursing home's history, I would never have admitted Mom." It was that comment, similar comments and countless other stories of distraught families that motivated me to write this book. I love and enjoy what I do. But unfortunately, by the time a family comes to see me, the damage has already been done.

Going Home

This book was written for these families. If it can prevent even one unfortunate circumstance, I will have accomplished my goal. For Betty, I believe we made a big difference in her life. The night before closing arguments I got a call from the opposing lawyer with a large settlement offer - about 15 times the amount we were offered prior to trial. I didn't think it was enough based on the facts of this case, and I firmly believed that the jury was very upset with this nursing home.

But I had to advise my client to take the offer. After all, Betty wanted "to go home." The offer and settlement were much more than the cost of her nearly $100,000 per year in-home care that she would need for the rest of her life. We settled. Betty went home. Her quality of life at home was much better than it was in the nursing home.

Of course, after talking to jurors we believed the jury would've awarded much more. But for Betty, a large verdict, subsequent appeals, and long protracted litigation would do nothing toward accomplishing her goal – "I want to go home."

7 Steps To Keep Your Loved One Safe In A Nursing Home … And *What To Do If Injured*, are dedicated to Aunt Betty, the aunt I never knew, and the countless other victims of nursing home abuse and neglect.

GETTING STARTED
ENSURE GOOD NURSING HOME CARE

Hopefully you spent a lot of time choosing the right nursing home for your loved one and utilized my book, *How to Select a Nursing Home for a Loved One*, as a guide. However, the process does not end when he or she moves into the home. Now the real work, and I do mean work, begins. The staff, administration, and owners can change, as can policies and procedures. It is important to stay involved and knowledgeable about the nursing home so you will continue to feel safe, secure, and happy about having a loved one there.

Families should be engaged in the care provided. It is a good idea to conduct your own formal review once or twice a year. Print out the "Review Nursing Home Checklist" (in the chapter titled HELPFUL RESOURCES) as you work through this chapter. This review will help you ensure good nursing home care. See the chapter titled KNOW THE RESIDENT'S RIGHTS to learn more about the specific rights your loved one has as a resident of a nursing home.

The bottom line is – you can't prevent all abuse or neglect as a relative, friend, or power of attorney. But you can absolutely go to bed every night knowing you've done your very best to keep your loved one safe in a nursing home. After all, it's supposed to be their home.

STEP 1: BE A ZEALOUS & VIGILANT ADVOCATE

Residents and family members who are concerned about the quality of life in a nursing home have formed Resident and Family Councils. They generally meet monthly or quarterly to plan special events, address issues of interest and concern, and discuss care questions with the staff and administration. Join! It's the equivalent of your child's Parent Teacher Organization (PTO).

These councils can also represent nursing home residents with the local and state legislature. For example, they can organize letter-writing campaigns to legislators when a bill concerning nursing home residents is pending before Congress.

If your nursing home does not have a council, suggest forming one. The council will relay quality-of-care concerns to the nursing home. If it's a good facility, it will work hand in hand with the resident's council.

STEP 2: THE PLAN OF CARE - THE RECIPE! IS IT BEING FOLLOWED?

What is it? It's much like Great Grandma's famous family recipe. All the right ingredients bring about a fabulous result. The Plan of Care is no different. State and federal regulations require a nursing home to establish a Plan of Care for each resident upon admission, and then reassess the resident's Plan of Care at least once each quarter or earlier, if the resident has experienced a significant change of condition.

The process is a multi-disciplinary approach and involves assessments from nurses, nurse aides, doctors, speech therapists, physical therapists, occupational therapists, social workers, administration, and most importantly FAMILY. Yes, the power of attorney has the right to participate in this process and MUST.

Most nursing homes will not necessarily tell you that you're allowed to participate. Simply inform the facility that you would like to attend. They should provide you with a date and time for such meeting. If it conflicts with your work schedule, request an alternative time. Any reasonable request should be accommodated.

The Plan of Care should be carefully and individually designed to benefit each nursing home resident. Ensure that the staff follows the Plan of Care. If you think of changes to make to the plan, document them so you can bring them forward at the regular Plan of Care review.

STEP 3: CONTINUE TO MONITOR THE FACILITY

You invested a lot of time and effort in choosing the best nursing home for your loved one. But now that he or she is settled, you need to remain vigilant. Administrators, owners, staff, procedures, and finances – changes in any of these factors and others can transform the nursing home you chose into one that is less than ideal.

This is especially important if your loved one becomes less able to communicate and/or move around. You should occasionally pull out the nursing home checklist from the chapter HELPFUL RESOURCES and note whether anything has changed in the nursing home since your initial visits.

A crucial factor in monitoring the home is visiting frequently and taking an active role in your loved one's care. You need to remain active in your communication with the staff to ensure that your loved one continues to receive proper care. Time and time again, insufficient numbers of nursing staff result in injuries that are otherwise preventable.

This usually results from the greedy aspect of the industry where nursing home operators place profits over patient care. Pop into the nursing home between 9 and 10 p.m. on occasion, and note the number of staff. Look around and note how long it takes staff to answer resident call lights. This is a tell-tale sign that the owner and/or administrator are cutting corners.

The Squeaky Wheel Gets Greased

This old adage is certainly true in nursing homes: Residents whose families are more involved receive more attention and better care. Make sure your loved one is one of those residents.

STEP 4: SUPPORT THE STAFF

Working in a nursing home can be stressful and tiring, and it is not typically highly paid. It's been my experience that the vast majority of people working on nursing staffs in these homes are well intentioned and conscientious people. In most cases, they too fall victim to the greedy nursing home corporation or owner. Show your appreciation to the staff members. Thank them for their acts of care and concern. Be sure to pass your compliments on to supervisors and administrators as well.

Acknowledge them with a card, cookies, or other small gestures. Trust me; this will go a long way to your loved one getting special consideration and treatment. It's human nature! When and if you need anything, these nurses will be of tremendous help.

STEP 5: COMMUNICATE AND COMMUNICATE MORE

Good communication between nursing home residents, family members, and staff leads to better overall care and a more peaceful living environment. Family members should talk to nursing home employees at every visit, just to check on how things are going and to learn about any changes in their loved one's behavior, attitude, or health. Nursing home residents should try to communicate changes in their feelings to the family and staff. And the family and staff should listen to the resident.

Improving Communication

Communication can be especially difficult between family members and residents with Alzheimer's, dementia, or other communication difficulties.

Try these tips to make communicating with these residents more successful:

1. Use effective body language. Sit at the resident's eye level, maintain eye contact, and keep your face cheerful and calm.

2. If a resident begins to talk about things unrelated to the conversation, let them speak. There may be a connection you don't yet understand.

3. Allow the resident time to understand what you are saying, rephrasing or repeating your words if necessary. However, do not allow them to struggle too long for words.

4. Try to reduce background noise, which can be distracting.

When Problems Occur

Nursing home residents and their families should be alert to potential problems and voice their concerns. When a resident or family member voices a concern, everyone must listen respectfully to each other and take complaints seriously.

Except in emergencies, work through the normal channels first. Try to resolve your issue by first discussing it with the nursing staff and then the Director of Nursing. If your issue is still not resolved to your satisfaction, speak with the Administrator. Document your concerns and the steps you have taken to resolve them (date, time, people involved, situation, and outcome) so you will be prepared if you ever need to escalate your complaint to the state Health Department, aging agency, or long-term care ombudsman.

You may also share concerns about menu and activity issues with the resident/family council. You should not discuss more significant issues with the resident/family council until you've exhausted the normal channels because nursing homes do not like when you discuss care issues with other paying customers.

File a CONFIDENTIAL Complaint if Necessary

Although good communication between residents, family members, and staff will hopefully resolve issues and problems in the early stages, it may sometimes be necessary to file a complaint. You should file a complaint when problems are serious or you have exhausted other channels to solve them. You can file a complaint about any aspect of care (such as staffing, safety, treatment, and so on) in licensed facilities.

If you are not sure how to file a complaint, start by calling your state's long-term care ombudsman — an "*ombudsman*" is a person that acts as a trusted intermediary between the state and its constituents, who investigates and attempts to resolve complaints. (Go to www.ltcombudsman.org/static_pages/ help.cfm and click on your state to get contact information for your ombudsman.) Your ombudsman will help you determine what to do next.

Although you may initially phone in your complaint, always follow up with a written version to ensure a paper trail. Use the notes you have made to write a brief, factual complaint.

Be sure to include the following information:

1. Name and address of the nursing home.

2. Your name, address, phone number, and relation to the resident.

3. Name of the resident on whose behalf the complaint is made.

4. Date(s) and time(s) of incidents.

5. Description of your specific complaints.

6. Names of witnesses (including other health care providers, such as hospital personnel).

7. Names of staff members, if relevant to the complaint.

8. Records that should be examined.

Families usually decide to file a complaint with the state licensing agency when other attempts fail, including when the ombudsman's route fails. Filing a complaint with the state licensing agency is serious and should be done only as a last resort. Most states maintain a confidential complaint hotline.

You can find your state's ombudsman, citizen groups and nursing home abuse hotlines in the final chapter of this book. After receiving a complaint, the agency follows up with an in-person inspection of the facility and its records concerning the issues outlined in the complaint.

Because four out of every five complaints filed are determined to be INVALID by the licensing agencies conducting complaint investigations, it is imperative that the complaint is detailed and factual. When filing a complaint, keep in mind the 5 Ws: Who, What, Where, When, and Why.

Explain the efforts you took to resolve the issue if it is

an ongoing concern. If you visit often, you can include information about other residents you have noticed that are not receiving adequate care — especially those who have no one to speak for them. Why? First, you are the voice for these residents. Second, by referencing others in your complaint, you make it very difficult for the nursing home to figure out who made the complaint.

If the state shows up to investigate one specific complaint about one specific resident, it's rather obvious for the nursing home to determine who made the complaint. Even though the state agency will not reveal your name, the facility will know who filed the complaint if only one specific person is named.

Also note that you should file a complaint if you observe abuse or neglect of other residents. Remember, your complaint to the state agency is confidential and your identity will not be revealed.

STEP 6: KEEP TRACK OF INSPECTIONS

When you initially evaluated potential nursing homes for your loved one, the regular state inspection was an important source of information you reviewed prior to choosing a home — as set forth in my book, *How to Select a Nursing Home for a Loved One.* Now that your loved one is actually settled in the nursing home, you should remain aware of inspections and periodically review the inspection reports. Don't forget to use the checklists in the HELPFUL RESOURCES section of this book.

This is a literal paper trail revealing the nursing home's ability to comply with state and federal regulations. The nursing home must make this information available to you whenever you request it. You can also request this information from your state agency by sending a written request under the Freedom of Information Act. Some states make this information available on the state department of health's (or equivalent agency's) website.

You may even be asked to participate in the inspection, as part of the inspection process involves interviews with residents and family members.

In addition, inspectors will:

1. Analyze the overall nursing home environment, including resident care and staff/resident interaction.
2. Review clinical records.
3. Interview caregivers and administrators.
4. Evaluate whether the nursing home meets individual resident needs.

5. Evaluate whether a nursing home meets standards for safe construction.

When an inspection team finds that a home does not meet a specific regulation, it issues a deficiency citation. Depending on the nature and severity of the problem, the state may:

1. Fine the nursing home.

2. Deny Medicare and Medicaid payments to the nursing home.

3. Assign a temporary manager.

4. Appoint a state monitor.

Just because a facility is cited doesn't mean your loved one is in a bad place. Review the findings and circumstances. Responsible nursing homes will review the deficiencies and take corrective action. You should become concerned when you see many investigators and/or deficiencies, particularly when the nursing home is cited repeatedly for the same deficiency code. This is a **BIG RED FLAG!**

Remember: Consult the "Survey" section of page 23 of my book, *How to Select a Nursing Home for a Loved One*, to refresh your memory on analyzing the scope and severity of deficiencies. If you don't have this book, you can request a copy at www.GreatInjuryLawyers.com. The nursing home has a chance to correct the deficiency. If it does not correct reported deficiencies, it can lose its license or certification to provide care to Medicare and Medicaid beneficiaries.

STEP 7: THE NEWSPAPER TRAIL

As mentioned before, understaffing is a huge problem in the elder care industry. Your local newspaper and online job postings can certainly be revealing. After your loved one enters a nursing home, you should monitor the want ads in the area where the nursing home is located. Check to see if the nursing home is advertising open positions for nurse aides, licensed practical nurses (LPNs), or registered nurses (RNs).

Monitor how often the ads appear because ongoing job postings can indicate understaffing. The same ad frequently appearing can indicate excessive staff turnover. Use this information and all other observations to monitor potential staffing problems that can lead to your loved one receiving substandard care.

HELPFUL RESOURCES

Use the checklists in this section to periodically re-evaluate the nursing home you choose to ensure it is still suitable for your loved one.

A good practice is to use these checklists yourself and provide them to anyone else that is helping you with this process. You should all independently use the checklists, and then compare notes after you've completed them. You should re-evaluate the nursing home at a minimum once a year but preferably twice a year.

Any time there is a change in ownership, you should also re-evaluate. When changes in ownership occur, this can be good or bad. Good if a new company is conscientious and dedicated to running a quality facility. Bad if the company operates the facility with a "profits over resident care" mindset. Take a look at the company's history in operating other nursing homes.

A vigilant and dedicated caretaker, family member, spouse or power of attorney can make all the difference in the world to the care your loved one receives.

Brad Lakin

NURSING HOME CHECKLIST
(adapted from www.medicare.gov)

Name of Nursing Home:_____

Date of Visit:_____

Basic Information			
Questions	Yes	No	Comments
The nursing home is Medicare-certified.			
The nursing home is Medicaid-certified.			
The nursing home has the level of care needed (e.g. skilled, custodial), and a bed is available.			
The nursing home has special services if needed in a separate unit (e.g. dementia, ventilator, or rehabilitation), and a bed is available.			
The nursing home is located close enough for friends and family to visit.			
Resident Appearance			
Questions	Yes	No	Comments

	Yes	No	Comments
Residents are clean, appropriately dressed for the season or time of day, and well groomed.			
Residents appear healthy and happy.			
Nursing Home Living Spaces			
Questions	Yes	No	Comments
The nursing home is free from overwhelming unpleasant odors.			
The nursing home appears clean and well kept.			
The temperature in the nursing home is comfortable for residents.			
The nursing home has good lighting.			
Noise levels in the dining room and other common areas are comfortable.			
Smoking is not allowed or may be restricted to certain areas of the nursing home.			
Furnishings are sturdy, yet comfortable and attractive.	.		
Staff			
Questions	Yes	No	Comments
The relationship between the staff and the residents appears to be warm, polite, and respectful.			

All staff members wear nametags.			
Staff members knock on the door before entering a resident's room and refer to residents by name.			
The nursing home offers a training and continuing education program for all staff.			
The nursing home does background checks on all staff.			
The guide on your tour knows the residents by name and is recognized by them.			
The home has a full-time Registered Nurse (RN) present all times, other than the Administrator or Director of Nursing.			
The same team of nurses and Certified Nursing Assistants (CNAs) work with the same resident 4 to 5 days per week.			
CNAs work with a reasonable number of residents.			
CNAs are involved in care planning meetings.			
The staff includes a full-time social worker.			
The staff has a licensed doctor. Is he or she there daily? Can he or she be reached at all times?			

The nursing home's management team has worked together for at least one year.			
Key staff members work full-time rather than part-time.			
There is an adequate ratio of nurses and certified nursing assistants per number of residents.			
Residents' Rooms			
Questions	Yes	No	Comments
Residents may have personal belongings and/or furniture in their rooms.			
The home has safety features such as railings and grab bars in residents' rooms and bathrooms.			
Each resident has storage space (closet and drawers) in his or her room.			
Each bedroom has a window.			
Residents have access to a personal telephone and television.			
Residents have a choice of roommates.			
Residents can reach water pitchers.			
The home has policies and procedures to protect a resident's possessions.			

Hallways, Stairs, Lounges, and Bathrooms			
Questions	Yes	No	Comments
Exits are clearly marked.			
There are quiet areas where residents can visit with friends and family.			
The nursing home has smoke detectors and sprinklers.			
All common areas, resident rooms, and doorways are designed for wheelchair use.			
The home has handrails in the hallways and grab bars in the bathrooms.			
Hallways are kept clear of obstructions such as housekeeping carts.			
Menus and Food			
Questions	Yes	No	Comments
Residents have a choice of food items at each meal. (Ask whether favorite foods are served.)			
Nutritious snacks are served twice daily			
Staff help residents eat and drink at mealtimes if help is needed.			

Activities			
Questions	Yes	No	Comments
Residents, including those who are unable to leave their rooms, may choose to take part in a variety of activities.			
The home offers a variety of activities for residents to choose from.			
The nursing home has outdoor areas for resident use, and staff members help residents go outside.			
The nursing home has an active volunteer program.			
Safety and Care			
Questions	Yes	No	Comments
The nursing home has an emergency evacuation plan and conducts regular fire drills.			
Residents get preventive care, such as a yearly flu shot, to help keep them healthy.			
Residents may still see their personal doctors.			
The nursing home has an arrangement with a nearby hospital for emergencies.			

Care plan meetings are scheduled at times that are convenient for residents and family members to attend whenever possible.			
The nursing home has corrected all deficiencies (failure to meet one or more federal or state requirements) on its last state inspection report, or has a plan in place to correct these deficiencies.			
The building includes fire extinguishers, smoke detectors, carbon monoxide detectors, and a sprinkler system.			
The home has emergency plans to deal with natural disasters.			

State Surveys and Complaint History			
Questions	Yes	No	Comments
A survey and complaint notebook is available. (note dates of surveys and complaint investigation for future)			
The home has a history of deficiencies.			
The home has a history of complaints that have been investigated by the state.			
Any of the complaints or deficiencies involve: Bedsores			

Infections Falls Malnutrition Dehydration Failure to medicate Failure to monitor Assault Staffing Failure to conduct background checks on employees			
The nursing home has corrected all deficiencies (failure to meet one or more federal or state requirements) on its last state inspection report, or a plan is in place to correct these deficiencies.			
Additional Comments:			

NURSING HOME REVIEW CHECKLIST

Resident or Family Council			
Questions	Yes	No	Comments
The nursing home has a Resident or Family Council that meets regularly.			
Staff and administration are open to suggestions and ideas developed by the Resident or Family Council.			
Plan of Care			
Questions	Yes	No	Comments
The staff is following the Plan of Care.			
The Plan of Care is reviewed regularly to make necessary adjustments.			
The resident or family feels included in Plan of Care process.			
Monitor the Facility			
Questions	Yes	No	Comments
The nursing home continues to feel safe, clean, and comfortable.			

Staff members are caring and concerned.			
My loved one receiving care/attention.			

Staff and Communication			
Questions	Yes	No	Comments
Staff members are willing to talk to me about my loved one's care			
Staff members keep me informed about any changes in my loved one's health, behavior, eating habits, etc.			

Inspections			
Questions	Yes	No	Comments
I have reviewed the latest nursing home inspection report.			
The nursing home is correcting all deficiencies (failure to meet one or more federal or state requirements) on its last state inspection report, or has a plan to correct these deficiencies.			

Monitor the Local Paper			
Questions	Yes	No	Comments
The nursing home advertises for new staff members frequently.			
The nursing home has run the same ad for more than three weeks.			

Brad Lakin

Additional Comments:

KNOW THE RESIDENT'S RIGHTS
NURSING HOME RESIDENT RIGHTS

Nursing home residents have patient rights and certain protections under the law. The federal Nursing Home Reform Amendments of 1987, and corresponding state laws, protect residents in nearly all nursing facilities. This law requires that nursing facilities "promote and protect the rights of each resident." The resident's rights must be displayed in the nursing facility along with a contact number for the state's Long-Term Care Ombudsman.

GENERAL GOALS OF THE LAW

The general goals of the Nursing Home Reform Amendments law are fourfold:

1. Quality of life
2. Provision of services and activities
3. Participation in facility/home administration.
4. Access to the Ombudsman Program.

Quality of Life

The law requires nursing homes to "care for the residents in such a manner and in such an environment as will promote maintenance or enhancement of the quality of life of each resident." A new emphasis is placed on dignity, choice, and self-determination for nursing home residents.

Provision of Services and Activities

The law requires each nursing home to provide services and activities to attain or maintain the highest practicable physical, mental, and psychosocial well-

being of each resident in accordance with a written Plan of Care that is initially prepared, with participation to the extent practicable of the resident or the resident's legal representative.

Participation in Home Administration

The law makes "resident and advocate participation" part of the criteria for assessing a home's compliance with administration requirements.

Access to the Ombudsman Program

The law grants immediate access by ombudsmen to residents and reasonable access, in accordance with state law, by ombudsmen to records; requires homes to inform residents how to get in touch with ombudsmen to voice complaints, or in the event of a transfer or discharge from the home; and requires state agencies to share inspection results with ombudsmen. Your contact with the ombudsman is confidential.

SPECIFIC RESIDENT RIGHTS
Right to Self-Determination

Nursing home residents have the rights to:
1. Choose their personal physician.
2. Get full information, in advance, and participate in planning and making any changes in their care and treatment.
3. Reside and receive services with reasonable

accommodation by the home of individual needs and preferences.

4. Voice grievances about care or treatment they do or do not receive, without discrimination or reprisal, and to receive prompt response from the home.

5. Organize and participate in resident groups (and their families have the right to organize family groups) in the home.

Personal and Privacy Rights
Nursing home residents have the rights to:

1. Participation in social, religious, and community activities as they choose.

2. Privacy in medical treatment, accommodations, personal visits, written and telephone conversations, and meetings of resident and family groups.

3. Confidentiality of personal and clinical records.

Rights Regarding Abuse and Restraints
Nursing home residents have the rights to:

1. Be free from physical or mental abuse, corporal punishment, involuntary seclusion, or disciplinary use of restraints.

2. Be free of restraints used for the convenience of the staff

3. Have restraints used only under written physician's orders to treat a resident's medical symptoms and

4. to ensure the resident's safety and the safety of others.

5. Be given psychopharmacologic medication only as ordered by a physician as a part of a written Plan of Care for a specific medical symptom, with annual review for appropriateness by an independent, external expert.

Rights to Information
Nursing homes must:

1. Upon request provide residents with the latest inspection results and any plan of correction submitted by the home.

2. Notify residents in advance of any plans to change their rooms or roommate.

3. Inform residents of their rights upon admission and provide a written copy of the rights, including their rights regarding personal funds and their right to file a complaint with the state survey agency.

4. Inform residents in writing, at admission and throughout their stay, of the services available under the basic rate and of any extra charges for extra services, including, for Medicaid residents, a list of services covered by Medicaid and those for which there is an extra charge.

5. Prominently display and provide oral and written information for residents about how to apply for and use Medicaid benefits and how to receive a refund for previous private payments that Medicaid will pay retroactively.

Right to Visits

The nursing home must:

1. Permit immediate visits by a resident's personal physician and by representatives from the licensing agency and the Ombudsman Program.

2. Permit immediate visits by a resident's relatives, with the resident's consent.

3. Permit visits "subject to reasonable restriction" for others who visit with the resident's consent.

4. Permit ombudsmen to review resident's clinical records if a resident grants permission.

Transfer and Discharge Rights

1. Nursing homes "must permit each resident to remain in the facility and must not transfer or discharge the resident unless".

2. The transfer or discharge is necessary to meet the resident's welfare because the home cannot do so.

3. The transfer or discharge is appropriate because the resident's health has improved such that the resident no longer needs nursing home care.

4. The health or safety of other residents is endangered.

5. The resident has failed, after reasonable notice, to pay an allowable facility charge for an item or service provided upon the resident's request.

6. The home ceases to operate.

Residents and their representatives must be notified of a transfer at least 30 days in advance, or as soon as possible if more immediate changes in health require more immediate transfer. **In addition, the resident must be told:**

1. The reason for the transfer.

2 . His or her right to appeal the transfer.

3. The name, address, and phone number of the

Ombudsman Program and protection and advocacy programs for the mentally ill and developmentally disabled.

4. Their right to request that their bed be held, including information about how many days Medicaid will pay for the bed to be held and the facility's bed-hold policies, and the right to return to the next available bed if Medicaid bed-holding coverage lapses.

5. A home must also prepare and orient residents to ensure a safe and orderly transfer or discharge.

Protection of Personal Funds

A nursing home must not require residents to deposit their personal funds with the home. **If it does accept written responsibility for a resident's funds, the nursing home must:**

1. Keep funds totaling more than $50 in an interest-bearing account, separate from the home's account.

2. Keep other funds available in a separate account or petty cash fund.

3. Keep a complete and separate accounting of each resident's funds, with a written record of all transactions, available for review by residents and

their representatives.

4. Notify Medicaid residents when their account balance comes within $200 of the Medicaid limit and the effect of this on their eligibility.

5. Upon a resident's death, turn funds over to the resident's trustee.

6. Purchase a surety bond to secure residents' funds in its keeping.

7. Not charge a resident for any item or service covered by Medicaid, specifically including routine personal hygiene items and services.

Protection Against Medicaid Discrimination
Nursing homes must:

1. Establish and maintain identical policies and practices regarding transfer, discharge and the provision of services required under Medicaid for all individuals regardless of source of payment.

2. Not require residents to waive their rights to Medicaid, and must provide information about how to apply for Medicaid.

3. Not require a third party to guarantee payment as a condition of admission or continued stay.

4. Not "charge, solicit, accept or receive" gifts,

money, donations or "other consideration" as a precondition for admission or for continued stay by people eligible for Medicaid.

WHO TO CONTACT RESOURCES

This section contains valuable information from three general resources: Ombudsmen, Citizen Groups, and Nursing Home Abuse Hotlines.

There is an Ombudsman in each state who is the person assigned to be the go-between with the nursing home on various issues, including resident care. The level of assistance you receive from Ombudsmen can vary drastically from state to state depending on the power asserted by the nursing home industry within the state.

Various Citizen Groups in each state serve a great role in advocating for nursing home residents on various issues. These organizations can be valuable in the process of selecting nursing homes because they often hear of the facilities that provide poor care.

When you are faced with the unfortunate circumstance of reported abuse to the state hotline regarding your loved one or another resident, make sure to always note circumstances of more than just your loved one. This is for two reasons. First, if you complain about more than just one person, the likelihood that a thorough investigation will be conducted increases.

Second, by referencing another resident the nursing home will be less likely to figure out who reported the neglect to the confidential hotline. If you only report your loved one, it's easy for the nursing home to determine who made the report.

All three sections have state-by-state resources.

OMBUDSMEN

Alabama

Virginia Moore-Bell
State LTC Ombudsman
AL Dept. of Senior Services
770 Washington Avenue
RSA Plaza, Suite 470
Montgomery, AL 36130
Tel: (334) 242-5743
Fax: (334) 242-5594
Website: http://www.alabamaageline.gov/ltc.cfm

Alaska
Robert Dreyer
State LTC Ombudsman
Office of the State LTC Ombudsman
AK Mental Health Trust Auth.
550 West 7th Avenue

Suite 1830
Anchorage, AK 99501
Tel: (907) 334-4480
Fax: (907) 334-4486
Website: http://www.akoltco.org

Arizona
Robert Nixon
State LTC Ombudsman
AZ Aging & Adult Administration
1789 West Jefferson
#950-A
Phoenix, AZ 85007
Tel: (602) 542-6454
Fax: (602) 542-6575
Website: https://www.azdes.gov/daas/ltco/

Arkansas
Kathie Gately
State LTC Ombudsman
AR Division of Aging & Adult Services
P.O.B. 1437
Slot S530
Little Rock, AR 72203-1437
Tel: (501) 682-8952
Fax: (501) 682-8155
Website: http://www.arombudsman.com/

California
Joe Rodrigues
State LTC Ombudsman
CA Department on Aging
1300 National Drive
Suite 200
Sacramento, CA 95834
Tel: (916) 419-7510

Brad Lakin

Fax: (916) 928-2503
Website: http://www.aging.ca.gov/Programs/LTCOP/

Colorado
Pat Tunnell
State LTC Ombudsman
The Legal Center
455 Sherman Street
Suite 130
Denver, CO 80203
Tel: (800) 288-1376
Fax: (303) 722-0720
Website: http://www.thelegalcenter.org/index.php?s=10298

Connecticut
Maggie Ewald
Acting State LTC Ombudsman
Office of the State LTC Ombudsman
CT Department of Social Services
25 Sigourney Street
12th Floor
Hartford, CT 06106-5033
Tel: (860) 424-5200
Fax: (860) 424-4808
Website: http://www.ltcop.state.ct.us/

Delaware
Beverly Morris
Acting State LTC Ombudsman
Division of Services for Aging & Adults
1901 North Dupont Highway
Main Admin. Bldg. Annex
New Castle, DE 19720
Tel: (302) 255-9390
Fax: (302) 255-4445
Website: http://dhss.delaware.gov/dhss/main/ltcop.html

District of Columbia
Gerald Kasunic
State LTC Ombudsman
Legal Counsel for the Elderly
601 E Street, N.W.
A4-315
Washington, DC 20049
Tel: (202) 434-2140
Fax: (202) 434-6595
Website: http://www.aarp.org/states/dc/LCE.html

Florida
Brian Lee
State LTC Ombudsman
Department of Elder Affairs
Florida State LTC Ombudsman Council
4040 Esplanade Way
Tallahassee, FL 32399
Tel: (888) 831-0404
Fax: (850) 414-2377
Website: http://ombudsman.myflorida.com/

Georgia
Becky Kurtz
State LTC Ombudsman
Office of the State LTCO
2 Peachtree Street, NW
9th Floor
Atlanta, GA 30303-3142
Tel: (888) 454-5826
Fax: (404) 463-8384
Website: http://www.georgiaombudsman.org

Hawaii
John McDermott

State LTC Ombudsman
Executive Office on Aging
250 South Hotel Street
Suite 406
Honolulu, HI 96813-2831
Tel: (808) 586-0100
Fax: (808) 586-0185
Website: http://hawaii.gov/health/eoa/LTCO.html

Idaho
Cathy Hart
State LTC Ombudsman
Idaho Commission on Aging
P.O. Box 83720
3380 American Terrace, Suite 120
Boise, ID 83720-0007
Tel: (208) 334-3833
Fax: (208) 334-3033
Website:
http://www.idahoaging.com/ombudsman/index.html

Illinois
Sally Petrone
State LTC Ombudsman
Illinois Department on Aging
421 East Capitol Avenue
Suite 100
Springfield, IL 62701-1789
Tel: (217) 785-3143
Fax: (217) 524-9644
Website: http://www.state.il.us/aging

Iowa
Jeanne Yordi
State LTC Ombudsman
Iowa Department of Elder Affairs

Clemens Building
200 10th Street, 3rd Floor
Des Moines, IA 50309-3609
Tel: (515) 242-3327
Fax: (515) 242-3300
Website:
http://www.aging.iowa.gov/advocacy/ombudsman.html

Indiana
Arlene Franklin
State LTC Ombudsman
Indiana Division Disabilities\Rehab Services
402 W. Washington St., Room W 454
PO Box 7083, MS21
Indianapolis, IN 46207-7083
Tel: (800) 545-7763
Fax: (317) 232-7867
Website: http://www.in.gov/fssa/da/3474.htm

Kansas
Kathy Greenlee
State LTC Ombudsman
Office of the State LTC Ombudsman
900 SW Jackson Street
Suite 1041
Topeka, KS 66612
Tel: (785) 296-3017
Fax: (785) 296-3916
Website: http://www.kansasombudsmanksgov.com/

Kentucky
Charles Smith
State LTC Ombudsman
Office of the Ombudsman
Cabinet for Health & Family Services
275 East Main Street

1E-B
Frankfort, KY 40621
Tel: (502) 564-5497
Fax: (502) 564-9523
Website: http://cfc.ky.gov/agencies/Ombudsman/

Louisiana
Linda Sadden
State LTC Ombudsman
Office of Elderly Affairs
412 N. 4th Street, 3rd Floor
P.O. Box 61
Baton Rouge, LA 70821
Tel: (225) 342-6872
Fax: (225) 342-7144
Website:
http://wwwprd.doa.louisiana.gov/laservices/publicpages/Se
rviceDetail.cfm?service_id=2803

Maine
Brenda Gallant
State LTC Ombudsman
Maine LTC Ombudsman Program
1 Weston Court
P.O. Box 128
Augusta, ME 04332
Tel: (207) 621-1079
Fax: (207) 621-0509
Website: http://www.maineombudsman.org

Maryland
Patricia Bayliss
State LTC Ombudsman
Maryland Department of Aging
301 W. Preston Street
Room 1007

Baltimore, MD 21201
Tel: (410) 767-1091
Fax: (410) 333-7943
Website: http://www.aging.maryland.gov/senior.html

Massachusetts
Mary McKenna
State LTC Ombudsman
Massachusetts Exec Office of Elder Affairs
1 Ashburton Place
5th Floor
Boston, MA 02108-1518
Tel: (617) 727-7750
Fax: (617) 727-9368
Website: http://www.mass.gov/elders/service-orgs-
advocates/ltc-ombudsman/ltc-ombudsman-overview.html

Michigan
Sarah Slocum
State LTC Ombudsman
Michigan Office of Services to the Aging
7109 West Saginaw
P.O. Box 30676
Lansing, MI 48909
Tel: (517) 335-0148
Fax: (517) 373-4092
Website: http://www.michigan.gov/miseniors/0,4635,7-
234-49992-191521--,00.html

Minnesota
Jean Wood
Acting State LTC Ombudsman
Office of Ombudsman for Older Minnesotans
121 East Seventh Place
Suite 410
St. Paul, MN 55101

Brad Lakin

Tel: (651) 296-0382
Fax: (651) 297-5654
Website: http://www.mnaging.org.

Mississippi
Anniece McLemore
State LTC Ombudsman
State LTC Ombudsman
MS Dept. of Human Services, Div. of Aging
750 North State Street
Jackson, MS 39202
Tel: (601) 359-4927
Fax: (601) 359-9664
Website: http://www.mdhs.state.ms.us

Missouri
Carol Scott
State LTC Ombudsman
Department of Health & Senior Services
P.O. Box 570
Jefferson City, MO 65102
Tel: (800) 309-3282
Fax: (573) 526-4314
Website: http://health.mo.gov/seniors/ombudsman/

Montana
Kelly Moorse
State LTC Ombudsman
MT Dept. of Health & Human Services
P.O. Box 4210
111 N. Sanders
Helena, MT 59604-4210
Tel: (800) 551-3191
Fax: (406) 444-7743
Website:
http://www.dphhs.mt.gov/sltc/services/aging/ltcombudsma

n.shtml

Nebraska
Cindy Kadavy
State LTC Ombudsman
Division of Aging Services
P.O. Box 95044
Lincoln, NE 68509-5044
Tel: (402) 471-2307
Fax: (402) 471-4619
Website:
http://dhhs.ne.gov/medicaid/Pages/ags_ltcombud.aspx

Nevada
Kay Panelli
State Long-Term Care Ombudsman
Nevada Division for Aging Services
445 Apple Street
Suite 104
Reno, NV 89502
Tel: (775) 688-2964
Fax: (775) 688-2969
Website: http://www.nvaging.net/ltc.htm

New Hampshire
Don Rabun
State LTC Ombudsman
NH LTC Ombudsman Program
129 Pleasant Street
Concord, NH 03301-3857
Tel: (603) 271-4704
Fax: (603) 271-5574
Website: http://www.dhhs.nh.gov/oltco/index.htm

New Jersey
William Isele
State LTC Ombudsman
Office of Ombudsman for Institutional Elderly
P.O. Box 807
Trenton, NJ 08625-0807
Tel: (609) 943-4026
Fax: (609) 943-3479
Website: http://www.nj.gov/ooie/

New Mexico
Walter Lombardi
State LTC Ombudsman
New Mexico Aging & LTC Services Dept.
1015 Tijeras Avenue, N.W.
Suite 200
Albuquerque, NM 87102
Tel: (505) 222-4500
Fax: (505) 222-4526

New York
Martha Haase
State LTC Ombudsman
New York State Office for the Aging
2 Empire State Plaza
Agency Building #2

Albany, NY 12223
Tel: (518) 474-7329
Fax: (518) 474-7761
Website: http://www.ltcombudsman.ny.gov/

North Carolina
Sharon Wilder
State LTC Ombudsman
NC Division of Aging & Adult Services

2101 Mail Service Center
Raleigh, NC 27699-2101
Tel: (919) 733-8395
Fax: (919) 715-0868
Website: http://www.dhhs.state.nc.us/aging/ombud.htm

North Dakota
Helen Funk
State LTC Ombudsman
Long Term Care Ombudsman Prog.
Aging Services Division
600 E. Boulevard Avenue
Dept. 325
Bismarck, ND 58505
Tel: (800) 451-8693
Fax: (701) 328-4061
Website:
http://www.nd.gov/dhs/services/adultsaging/ombudsman.ht
ml

Ohio
Beverley Laubert
State LTC Ombudsman
Ohio Department of Aging
50 W Broad Street
9th Floor
Columbus, OH 43215-3363
Tel: (614) 466-1221
Fax: (614) 644-5201
Website: http://www.goldenbuckeye.com

Oklahoma
Esther Houser
State LTC Ombudsman
Long Term Care Ombudsman Prog.
DHS Aging Services Division

2401 N.W. 23rd Street
Suite 40
Oklahoma City, OK 73107
Tel: (405) 521-6734
Fax: (405) 522-6739
Website:
http://www.okdhs.org/divisionsoffices/visd/asd/ltc/

Oregon
Meredith Cote
State LTC Ombudsman
Oregon Office of the LTC Ombudsman
3855 Wolverine NE
Suite 6
Salem, OR 97305-1251
Tel: (503) 378-6533
Fax: (503) 373-0852
Website: http://www.oregon.gov/ltco/index.shtml

Pennsylvania
Wilmarie Gonzalez
State LTC Ombudsman
Pennsylvania Department of Aging
555 Walnut Street, 5th Floor
P.O. Box 1089
Harrisburg, PA 17101
Tel: (717) 783-1550
Fax: (717) 772-3382
Website:
http://www.portal.state.pa.us/portal/server.pt/community/ad
vocacy_(ombudsman)/19389

Rhode Island
Roberta Hawkins
State LTC Ombudsman

Alliance for Better Long Term Care
422 Post Road
Suite 204
Warwick, RI 02888
Tel: (401) 785-3340
Fax: (401) 785-3391
Website:
http://adrc.ohhs.ri.gov/livingathome/long_term.php

South Carolina
Jon Cook
State LTC Ombudsman
SC DHHS, Office on Aging
1301 Gervais Street
Suite 200
Columbia, SC 29201
Tel: (803) 734-9900
Fax: (803) 734-9886
Website:
http://aging.sc.gov/seniors/ombudsman/Pages/index.aspx

South Dakota
Jeff Askew
State LTC Ombudsman
Department of Social Services
SD Office of Adult Services & Aging
700 Governors Drive
Pierre, SD 57501-2291
Tel: (605) 773-3656
Fax: (605) 773-6834
Website:
http://www.state.sd.us/social/ASA/services/ombudsman.htm

Tennessee
Adrian Wheeler
State LTC Ombudsman

TN Commission on Aging and Disability
Andrew Jackson Bldg.
500 Deaderick Street, Ste. 825
Nashville, TN 37243
Tel: (615) 741-2056
Fax: (615) 741-3309
Website:
http://www.state.tn.us/comaging/ombudsman.html

Texas
John Willis
State LTC Ombudsman
State Long Term Care Ombudsman Prog.
Texas Department of Aging and Disability Serv
701 West 51st Street
P.O. Box 149030, Mail Code: 250
Austin, TX 78714-9030
Tel: (512) 438-4356
Fax: (512) 438-4374
Website: www.dads.state.tx.us/news_info/ombudsman
Utah
Chad McNiven
State LTC Ombudsman
Department of Human Services
Utah Division of Aging & Adult Services
120 North 200 West
Room 325
Salt Lake City, UT 84103
Tel: (801) 538-3910
Fax: (801) 538-4395
Website: http://daas.utah.gov/ombudsman/index.html

Vermont
Jacqueline Majoros
State LTC Ombudsman
Vermont Legal Aid, Inc.

264 N. Winooski Avenue
P.O. Box 1367
Burlington, VT 05402
Tel: (802) 863-5620
Fax: (802) 863-7152
Website: http://www.vtlegalaid.org/our-projects/vermont-long-term-care-ombudsman/

Virginia
Joani Latimer
State LTC Ombudsman
VA Association of Area Agencies on Aging
24 E. Cary Street
Suite 100
Richmond, VA 23219
Tel: (804) 565-1600
Fax: (804) 644-5640
Website: http://www.vaaaa.org

Washington
Kary Hyre
State LTC Ombudsman
Multi-Service Center
1200 South 336th Street
P.O. Box 23699
Federal Way, WA 98093
Tel: (800) 422-1384
Fax: (253) 815-8173
Website: http://www.ltcop.org/index.htm

West Virginia
Larry Medley
State LTC Ombudsman
West Virginia Bureau of Senior Services

1900 Kanawha Boulevard East
Bldg #10
Charleston, WV 25305-0160
Tel: (304) 558-3317
Fax: (304) 558-0004
Website: http://www.state.wv.us/seniorservices/

Wisconsin
George Potaracke
State LTC Ombudsman
Wisconsin Board on Aging & Long Term Care
1402 Pankratz Street
Madison, WI 53704-4001
Tel: (800) 815-0015
Fax: (608) 246-7001
Website:
http://www.dhs.wisconsin.gov/aging/boaltc/ltcombud.htm

Wyoming
Deborah Alden
State LTC Ombudsman
Wyoming Senior Citizens, Inc
756 Gilchrist, P.O. Box 94
Wheatland, WY 82201
Tel: (307) 322-5553
Fax: (307) 322-3283
Website: http://www.wyomingseniors.com/services/long-
term-care-ombudsman

Guam
Evelyn Cruz
State LTC Ombudsman
Division of Senior Citizens, Guam DPHSS
P.O. Box 2816
Hagatna, GU 96932
Tel: (671) 735-7382

Fax: (671) 735-7416
Website: http://dphss.guam.gov/content/long-term-care-ombudsman-services-program
Puerto Rico
Carmen Matos
State LTC Ombudsman
Puerto Rico Governor's Office of Elder Affairs
Call Box 50063
Old San Juan Station
San Juan, PR 00902
Tel: (787) 725-1515
Fax: (787) 721-6510

CITIZEN GROUPS

Alabama
Alabama Advocates for Quality Care
3717 Midway Road
Adamsville, AL 35005
Contact: Dixie Kuykendall
ph: (205) 674-9853
e-mail: dixiek@charter.net

Arkansas
AR Advocates for Nursing Home Residents
961 Paul Drive
Conway, AR 72034
Contact: Nancy Allison
ph: (501) 327-3152
fax: (501) 884-6728
e-mail: info@aanhr.org
Website: http://www.aanhr.org

AR Advocates for Nursing Home Residents
P.O. Box 22421
Little Rock, AR 72221-2421

Brad Lakin

Contact: Virginia Cross
ph: (501) 225-4082
fax: (501) 884-6728

AR Advocates for Nursing Home Residents
135 Hillview Drive
Apt 112
Fairfield Bay, AR 72088
Contact: Nancy Johnson
ph: (501) 884-6728
fax: (501) 884-6728

California
Foundation Aiding the Elderly
P.O. Box 254849
Sacramento, CA 95865-4849
Contact: Carole Herman
ph: (916) 481-8558
fax: (916) 481-8329
e-mail: carole@4fate.org
Website: http://www.4fate.org

CA Advocates for Nursing Home Reform
650 Harrison Street
2nd Floor
San Francisco, CA 94107-1311
Contact: Patricia McGinnis
ph: (415) 974-5171
fax: (415) 777-2904
e-mail: PatM@canhr.org
Website: http://www.canhr.org

Connecticut
CT Citizens Coalition for NH Reform
211 State Street
Bridgeport, CT 06604

Contact: Steven Kilpatrick
ph: (203) 336-3851
fax: (203) 333-4976
e-mail: skilpatrick@connlegalservices.org
Advocates for Loved Ones in Nursing Homes
28 B Damon Heights Road
Niantic, CT 06357
Contact: Maryann Lidestri
e-mail: aflon@hotmail.com

Florida
Fighting Elder Abuse Together (FEAT)
1625 La Maderia Dr., S.W.

Palm Bay, FL 32908
Contact: Judy Ahler-Friddle
ph: (321) 984-8883
fax: (321) 956-7606
e-mail: ahler_friddle@msn.com

Coalition to Protect America's Elders
3699 Plowshare Road
Tallahassee, FL 32309
Contact: Barbara Hengstebeck
ph: (850) 216-2727
fax: (850) 216-1933
e-mail: coalitiontoprotect@comcast.net
Website: http://www.protectelders.org

Quality Care Advocates, Inc
P.O. Box 494224
Port Charlotte, FL 33949
Contact: Linda Pounds
ph: (941) 743-0987
e-mail: llpsterling@aol.com

Advocates Committed To Improving Our NH's
4714 W. Euclid Ave.
Tampa, FL 33629
Contact: Anna Spinella
ph: (813) 837-1714
e-mail: amspinel@tampabay.rr.com

Georgia
Georgia Council on Aging
2 Peachtree Street, NW
Atlanta, GA 30303
Contact: Melanie McNeil
ph: (404) 657-5348
fax: (404) 657-1722
e-mail: msmcneil@dhr.state.ga.us
Website: http://www.gcoa.org

Illinois
Nursing Home Monitors
6111 Vollmer Lane
Godfrey, IL 62035
Contact: Violette King
ph: (618) 466-3410
fax: (618) 466-3410
e-mail: vkmonitor@earthlink.net
Website: http://www.nursinghomemonitors.org

Illinois Citizens For Better Care
220 South State Street
Suite 1928
Chicago, IL 60604
Contact: Wendy Meltzer
ph: (312) 663-5120
fax: (312) 427-0181
e-mail: wmicbc@core.com

Tender Loving Care in Long Term Care
620 North Walnut St.
Springfield, IL 62702
Contact: Margaret Niederer
ph: (217) 523-8488
fax: (217) 523-8493
e-mail: email@tlcinltc.org
Indiana
United Senior Action
324 W. Morris Street
Suite 114
Indianapolis, IN 46225-1491
Contact: Robyn Grant
ph: (317) 634-0872
fax: (317) 687-3661
e-mail: robyngrant@comcast.net

Kansas
Kansas Advocates for Better Care
913 Tennessee Street, #2
Lawrence, KS 66044
Contact: Deanne Bacco
ph: (800) 525-1782
fax: (785) 749-0029
e-mail: info@kabc.org
Website: http://www.kabc.org

Kentucky
Kentuckians for Nursing Home Reform
1530 Nicholasville Road
Lexington, KY 40503
Contact: Bernie Vonderheide
ph: (859) 312-5617
e-mail: kynursinghomereform@yahoo.com
Website: http://www.kynursinghomereform.org

Louisiana
Citizens Care
1321 8th Street
New Orleans, LA 70118
Contact: Doris Taylor
ph: (504) 896-8912
e-mail: citizens@citizenscare.org
Maryland
Voices for Quality Care (LTC)
PO Box 6555, US Postal Service
St. Charles Town Center Mall
Waldorf, MD 20603
Contact: Kate Ricks
ph: (888) 600-2375
e-mail: voicesforqualitycare@hotmail.com
Website: http://www.voicesforqualitycare.org

Massachusetts
MA Advocates for Nursing Home Reform
38 Banks Terrace
Swampscott, MA 01907
Contact: Arlene Germain
ph: (781) 890-2244
fax: (781) 890-4956
e-mail: agermain@matrixpartners.com
Website: http://www.manhr.org
Cape United Elders of Comm. Action Committee
115 Enterprise Road
Hyannis, MA 02601
Contact: Susan Walker
ph: (508) 771-1727
fax: (508) 775-7488
e-mail: susanw@cacci.cc

Michigan

Michigan Campaign for Quality Care
5886 Highgate Avenue
East Lansing, MI 48823
Contact: Alison Hirschel
ph: (517) 324-5754
fax: (517) 333-4339
e-mail: hirschel@umich.edu
Website: http://www.campaignforqualitycare.org
Citizens For Better Care
4750 Woodward Avenue
Suite 410
Detroit, MI 48201-1308
Contact: Nancy Jackson
ph: (313) 832-6387
fax: (313) 832-7407
e-mail: cbcnancyj@yahoo.com
Website: http://cbcmi.org

Minnesota
ElderCare Rights Alliance
2626 East 82nd Street
Suite 230
Bloomington, MN 55425
Contact: Tom Hyder
ph: (952) 854-7304
fax: (952) 854-8535
e-mail: thyder@eldercarerights.org

Missouri
Missouri Coalition for Quality Care
P.O. Box 7165
Jefferson City, MO 65102
Contact: Georgia Sanders
ph: (888) 262-5644
e-mail: mail@mcqc.com
Website: http://www.mcqc.com

Nebraska
Nebraska Advocates for Nursing Home Residents
10050 Regency Circle
Suite 525
Omaha, NE 68114
Contact: Bill Seidler
ph: (402) 397-3801
fax: (402) 397-3869
e-mail: bjseidler@qwest.net

New Mexico
New Mexicans for Quality Long Term Care
P.O. Box 1712
Belen, NM 87002
Contact: J.C. Beverly
ph: (505) 864-7534
fax: (505) 864-7377
e-mail: jcbeverly@msn.com

New York
Coalition of Institutionalized Aged and Disab
425 East 25th Street
New York, NY 10010
Contact: Geoff Lieberman
ph: (212) 481-7572
fax: (212) 481-5149
e-mail: ciadny@aol.com
Website: http://www.ciadny.org

Long Term Care Community Coalition
242 West 30th Street
Suite 306
New York, NY 10001
Contact: Richard Mollot
ph: (212) 385-0355

fax: (212) 239-2801
e-mail: richard@ltccc.org
Website: http://www.ltccc.org
FRIA
18 John Street
Suite 905
New York, NY 10038
Contact: Amy Paul
ph: (212) 732-5667
fax: (212) 732-6945
e-mail: apaul@fria.org
Website: http://www.fria.org/fria/

North Carolina
Friends of Residents In Long Term Care
883-C Washington St.
Raleigh, NC 27605
Contact: Bill Lamb
ph: (919) 782-1530
fax: (919) 782-1558
e-mail: friends@forltc.org
Website: http://www.forltc.org/cms/

Ohio
Families For Improved Care Inc.
P.O. Box 21398
Columbus, OH 43221-1355
Contact: Donald Greenberg
ph: (614) 459-8438
e-mail: fficgroup@aol.com

Oklahoma
Oklahomans for Improvement of NH Care
1423 Oakwood Drive
Norman, OK 73069-4446
Contact: JoAnna Deighton

ph: (405) 364-5004
fax: (405) 364-5004
e-mail: JADCD@aol.com

Pennsylvania
CARIE
100 N. 17th Street
Suite 600
Philadelphia, PA 19103
Contact: Diane Menio
ph: (215) 545-5728
fax: (215) 546-9963
e-mail: menio@carie.org
Website: http://www.carie.org

Rhode Island
Alliance for Better Long Term Care
422 Post Road
Suite 204
Warwick, RI 02888
Contact: Roberta Hawkins
ph: (401) 785-3340
fax: (401) 785-3391
e-mail: rhawkins@alliancebltc.org
Website: http://www.alliancebltc.com/page14.php

Texas
Texas Advocates for Nursing Home Residents
500 East Anderson Ln.
#234W
Austin, TX 78752
Contact: Beth Ferris
ph: (512) 719-4757
fax: (512) 719-5057
e-mail: bethferris@peoplepc.com

Texas Advocates for Nursing Home Residents
1015 Wavecrest Dr.
Houston, TX 77062
Contact: Gay Nell Harper
ph: (281) 488-5291
fax: (281) 480-4351
e-mail: sealbeem@aol.com

Texas Advocates for Nursing Home Residents
634 Green Cove Lane
Dallas, TX 75232
Contact: Lou O'Reilly
ph: (972) 572-6330
fax: (214) 376-7707
e-mail: oreillyl@swbell.net

Texans For The Improvement of Long-Term Care
4545 Cook Road, #303
Houston, TX 77072-1125
Contact: Sam Perlin
ph: (281) 933-4533
fax: (281) 498-6344
e-mail: sperlin@aol.com

Virginia
Citizens Committee to Protect the Elderly
407 Oakmears Crescent
Virginia Beach, VA 23462
Contact: Judith Allison
ph: (757) 518-8500
fax: (757) 518-8501
e-mail: citizenscommittee@citizenscommittee.org
Website: http://www.citizenscommittee.org/

TLC for Long Term Care
P.O. Box 523323

Springfield, VA 22152
Contact: Dale Belrose
ph: (703) 338-7333
fax: (866) 487-8470
e-mail: tlc4ltc@msn.com
Virginia Friends & Relatives of NH Residents
1426 Claremount Avenue
Richmond, VA 23227
Contact: Joani Latimer
ph: (804) 644-2804
fax: (804) 644-5640
e-mail: elderights@aol.com

Friends & Relatives of Nursing Home Residents

P.O. Box 551
Harrisonburg, VA 22803
Contact: Anne Scott See
ph: (540) 896-2741
fax: (540) 433-2202
e-mail: asbrls@hotmail.com

Washington
Family Advocates for NH Improvement
10955 W. Villa Monte Drive
Mukilteo, WA 98275
Contact: Mary Gorale
ph: (888) 647-3367
fax: (888) 647-3367
e-mail: fanhimg@aol.com

Resident Councils of Washington
220 E. Canyon View Road
Belfair, WA 98528
Contact: Sharon McIntyre

ph: (360) 275-8000
fax: (360) 277-0144
e-mail: rcwexec@residentcouncil.org
Wyoming
Concerned Citizens For Quality Nsg Home Care
811 Glenn Road
Casper, WY 82601
Contact: Virginia King
ph: (307) 266-6659
e-mail: eca@wyoming.com

NURSING HOME ABUSE HOTLINES

Alabama
1-800-458-7214
More Information
Alabama Department of Senior Services

Alaska
1-800-730-6393 (Toll free in Alaska)
Outside of Alaska: 907-334-4483

Arizona
1-SOS-ADULT or 1-877-767-2385
602-674-4200
TDD: 1-877-815-8390

Arkansas
1-800-582-4887
In Pulaski County: (501) 682-8425
Fax: (501) 682-1967, Attention Complaint Unit
E-mail: complaints.OLTC@arkansas.gov
More Information
Arkansas Office of Long Term Care, Complaints Unit
Arkansas Long Term Care Ombudsman

Brad Lakin

California
1-800-231-4024
More Information
California Long Term Care Ombudsman

Colorado
1-800-773-1366 or
1-800-886-7689, Ext. 2800
(303) 692-2800
E-mail: health.facilities@state.co.us
Fax: (303) 753-6214
More Information
Colorado Department of Public Health Nursing Home
Complaints Program

Connecticut
1-860-424-5241

Delaware
1-800-223-9074

District of Columbia
202-434-2140

Florida
1-800-96ABUSE or 1-800-962-2873

Georgia
1-800-878-6442
(404) 657-5728 (Metro-Atlanta)
More Information
Georgia Office of Regulatory Services

Guam
(671) 475-0268
After Hours: 671-646-4455

(evenings, weekends, holidays)

Hawaii
(808) 832-5115(Oahu)
(808) 243-5151 (Maui, Molokai, and Lanai)
(808) 241-3432 (Kauai)
(808) 933-8820 (East Hawaii)
(808) 327-6280 (West Hawaii)
More Information
Hawaii Long Term Care Ombudsman
(808) 586-0100

Idaho
1-877-471-2777

Illinois
1-800-252-4343 (Toll free in Illinois)
TTY: 1-800-547-0466
Outside of Illinois: 217-785-0321
More Information
Illinois Department on Aging

Indiana
1-800-992-6978 (Toll free in Indiana)
Outside of Indiana: 1-800-545-7763, Ext. 20135

Iowa
1 -800-686-0027 or
1-877-686-0027
More Information
Iowa Long Term Care Ombudsman
Iowa Department of Inspections and Appeals, Health
Facilities Division

Kansas

1-800-842-0078
1-877-662-8362 (Toll free in Kansas)
Outside of Kansas: 785-296-3017
More Information
Kansas Office of the State Long Term Care Ombudsman

Kentucky

Elder Abuse Hotline: 1-800-752-6200
Long Term Care Ombudsman: 1-800-372-2991
TTY (for hearing impaired): 1-800-627-4702
Attorney General's Patient Abuse Tip Line: 1-877-ABUSE
TIP (1-877-228-7384)
More Information
Office of the Attorney General Medicaid Fraud & Abuse
Control Division
Kentucky Office of Inspector General

Louisiana

1-800-259-4990 (Toll free in Louisiana)
Outside of Louisiana: (225) 342-9722
Adults With Disabilities (Ages 18-59)
1-800-898-4910

Maine

1-800-383-2441 (Toll free in Maine)
Local/Out-of-State TTY: (207) 287-9312
More Information
Maine Department of Health and Human Services

Maryland

1-800-917-7383 (Toll free in Maryland)
1-800-AGE-DIAL, Ext. 1091 (Toll free in Maryland)
Outside of Maryland: (410) 767-1091
More Information
Maryland Long Term Care Ombudsman/Elder Abuse

Massachusetts
1-800-462-5540
1-800-AGE-INFO (1-800-243-4636)
Massachusetts Attorney General's Elder Hotline: 1-888-
AG-ELDER
(1-888-243-5337)
TTY: (617) 727-0434

Michigan
1-800-882-6006
More Information
Michigan Bureau of Health Systems

Minnesota
1-800-333-2433
TDD/TYY: 1-800-627-3529

Mississippi
1-800-227-7308
1-800-222-8000 (Toll free in Mississippi)
Outside of Mississippi: (601) 359-4991

Missouri
1-800-392-0210

Montana
1-800-551-3191 (Toll free in Montana)
Outside of Montana: (406) 444-4077
More Information
Montana Senior & Long Term Care Division Ombudsman

Nebraska
1-800-652-1999 (Toll free in Nebraska)
Outside of Nebraska: (402) 595-1324

Nevada
1-800-992-5757 (Toll free in Nevada)
Outside of Nevada:
Carson City area: (775) 687-4210
Reno area: (775) 688-2964
Elko area: (775) 738-1966
Las Vegas area: (702) 486-3545

New Hampshire
1-800-442-5640 or (603) 271-4375
More Information
New Hampshire Office of the Long Term Care
Ombudsman

New Jersey
1-800-792-8820 (Toll free in New Jersey)
Outside of New Jersey: (609) 943-3473
E-mail: acs@doh.state.nj.us

New Mexico
1-800-797-3260 or
(505) 841-6100 (In Albuquerque)

New York
1-888-201-4563
E-Mail: nhintake@health.state.ny.us
ADULT CARE HOME COMPLAINTS
(866) 893-6772
More Information
New York State Department of Health
Nursing Homes
Adult Care Facilities

North Carolina
1-800-662-7030

North Dakota
1-800-451-8693
Ohio
1-800-342-0533
TDD: (614) 752-6490
Fax: (614) 728-9169
E-mail: HCComplaints@gw.odh.state.oh.us
More Information
Ohio Department of Health

Oklahoma
1-800-522-3511
Oregon
1-800-522-2602 or
(503) 378-6533
AGING/DEVELOPMENTAL DISABILITIES
1-800-866-406-4287 or
(503) 945-9495
More Information
Oregon Long Term Care Ombudsman
Oregon Department of Human Services Office

Pennsylvania
1-800-254-5164
More Information
Pennsylvania Department of Health

Rhode Island
(401) 785-3340
Fax: (401) 785-3391

South Carolina
(803) 898-2850

South Dakota

(605) 773-3656

Tennessee
1-888-APS-TENN or 1-888-277-8366

Texas
1-800-458-9858 (Toll free in Texas)
Outside of Texas: (512) 834-3784

Utah
1-800-371-7897 (Toll free in Utah)
Outside of Utah: (801) 264-7669
E-mail: vruesch@utah.gov
Vermont
1-800-564-1612
(802) 241-2345
Fax (802) 241-2358
More Information
APS Online Report Form
Vermont Department of Aging & Independent Living

Virginia
1-888-83-ADULT or 1-888-832-3858
Richmond area: (804) 371-0896

Washington
1-800-562-6078

West Virginia
1-800-352-6513

Wisconsin
1-800-815-0015 (Toll free in Wisconsin)
Outside of Wisconsin: (608) 246-7013
More Information
Wisconsin Long Term Care Ombudsman

Wyoming
(307) 777-6137 or (307) 777-7123
More Information
Wyoming Long Term Care Ombudsman

www.ingramcontent.com/pod-product-compliance
Lightning Source LLC
Chambersburg PA
CBHW071608170526
45166CB00003B/1027